Job Search Essentials 2.0

Finding Your Next Career Adventure

Jim Wilson

Published by PathForeWord
http://www.PathForeWord.com

Table of Contents

Introduction

In June 2013 I was advised that the position I'd held and the career that I'd built over the past 21 years was ended. Many of you have had similar experiences and some of you more than once. We're now told to expect this a number of times during our careers. For me, this was the first time in 50 years of working. Although, I'll note that I'd conducted many lay-offs during that career and always expected that it would come my turn at some point.

I, of course, had a number of thoughts and reactions. At the end of a fair bit of thought, I decided to re-wire instead of retire and to do so around a career encore in writing and consulting. My first step was to set up a blog on career adventures. I've called it PathForeWord, as it is a path, it moves forward, and it involves words. It is also primarily about career adventures and particularly about the job search.

As the blog continued to grow, in terms of followers and relevant content, I felt that I could pull together a short eBook and share that content in one place for the benefit of fellow job seekers. This is that eBook.

I'll further note that as I was pulling together this eBook, I began to realize how much content is devoted to getting your thoughts together around your career transition. This includes the nature of work, living life, and dealing with loss --- among others. In fact, a very high percentage of this book is about getting into the right attitude, only then does it dive into the nuts and bolts of the job search.

So don't expect right off the bat to get into writing super resumes or hitting it out of the park during your interviews, to continue the analogy. Rather, think about spending some time in the dugout or better yet watching the game. Use that time to gather your thoughts, consider the changes in your career, your next steps, and particularly how you find a balance between work and living your life.

I hope you find this book valuable on your own PathForeWord.

Working and Living Life

This section is devoted to getting your thoughts together around your work, your life, and your job search, in that order. This is the most important part of your job search. This topic represents the majority of this book. Getting your head around where you've been, where you're going, and how you're going to get there is essential to finding your PathForeWord.

Career Twists

The title of my blog is PathForeWord. In order to embark on any path moving forward, you need to have a beginning point. And it would be best if you spent some time considering that beginning point, fully assessing it before launching on that next journey. In an aside, it would be wise not to linger over that assessment or you'll lose time on your next journey. Another reason for the review is to see if there are any valid lessons to be learned to better inform your next journey. Sometimes there are lessons to be learned, but often so much of what may have happened is really out of your direct control. That, too, is good to determine before moving forward.

My beginning was a phone call on the weekend. I was traveling on vacation and wouldn't be back the next day to be a part of the 30+ reduction in force that was used to pave the way to outsource our department. At the time, and in retrospect, I felt that this was fortunate. I was able to process my new status in the calming and supportive surroundings of my family and spend some time driving back with my wife to talk things through. For those who experienced the mass reduction in force, my heart goes out to them for the very stressful situation they endured.

I do recall one of the more classy reductions in my experience. I was running a training development division. One of our military contracts was cancelled at the start of the Gulf War. We had to let 25 people go that week. The project manager called everyone into her office, handed out envelopes, turned to them and said, "I've got one, too. Let's see what it says." I worked with her on that announcement; giving her the space to do it the way she felt was appropriate. I admire her calm courage and I know her team members appreciated her approach and her support as they followed the path forward to their next journey.

I'm reminded of the technique of breathing into a paper bag. For the uninitiated, this is the recommended procedure for dealing with a panic attack. I didn't reach that stage but there were many times over the next several days/weeks that I needed to remind myself to breathe deeply and often.

The phrase "This too shall pass" has proven to be helpful in these situations. In fact, as I was cleaning out my office I came across a card that I'd had produced in an earlier turbulent time, a layoff and restructuring. On one side it had the phrase "This too shall pass" and on the other side the phrase

"When one door closes, another opens: but we often look so long and so regretfully upon the closed door that we do not see the one which has opened for us."

So yes, our careers have those extremely unpleasant twists. It's time to find that next PathForeWord and don't forget to take your paper bag with you as you stretch your boundaries and find that adventurous path that can maximize your potential.

Career Turns

The PathForeWord has a number of turns, not to mention those uphill and downhill sections. Adaptability is the current rule of the organizational world. I've found that adaptability comes from two key aspects — maintaining a positive can-do attitude and continuous learning of new ways of getting things done, new ways of working with people. Okay, maybe that's three.

Live as if you were to die tomorrow. Learn as if you were to live forever. Mahatma Gandhi

I like the quote above, living in the here and now along with always learning. Living in the here and now is the heart of adaptability. Maintaining that can-do attitude and positive outlook can literally turn around all those around you — who, in turn, support your own efforts at maintaining a positive outlook. I see this approach as a conscious choice. You can choose to look negatively at all the events you experience and all those around you. But to what purpose? You can also choose to look positively at the changes in your life and your workplace. Sometimes it takes quite a bit of looking to find that glimmer of hope. But I assure you it is there.

It also helps to have a sense of humor. I often like to use the old phrase "on the one hand, and on the other hand". For example, well on the one hand I'm out of work, but on the other hand I've got lots of time to reinvent myself. Another way to look at this is to try the old phrase "fake it 'til you make it." Over time, working diligently on building your positive attitude and living in the here and now, it will become who you are, thereby helping you and all those around you.

The second aspect is continuous learning. If you're going to be adaptable, you need to keep up with all the changes around you. This includes organizational changes (keeping up with how you get things accomplished in an ever-changing hierarchy and new procedures/processes) and technological changes as well as industry changes. What's happening with the technology tools we use to get our work done? How do we communicate in a world of Twitter and Text? Get after it so that you can help your organization move through these changes and help your career in the process.

I'll further note that the act of continuous learning is a tool in and of itself. As you move from one career turn to the next, you'll need to learn lots of things at each of those turns. Building your learning skills and proficiency can really come into play at those critical junctures — learning the new organization, the new boss, the new procedures — gee whiz, even the new route to work in the morning!

In my own case, I've done a great deal over the years to build an enduring positive, enthusiastic outlook. I've done this despite many personal family hardships and losses. Or perhaps, I've done it because of those loses. I feel that I've experienced true personal loss (although it can always get worse and many have it far worse). This, in turn, informs my perspective when a set back happens at work. I know that this is really relatively minor in the overall course of life events.

Building new skill sets has taken on new meaning for me and for most. With my formal education complete with two graduate degrees, it's now up to me to learn in a hands-on manner. Plus, there are few formal courses on social media and other topics. Instead, I feel that many of today's forms of learning need to happen by just jumping in and experiencing it along with everyone else who is pioneering the new communication systems, as just one example. Of course, there are workshops and other industry events, panel discussions, etc. There are also some fabulous Massive Open Online Courses (MOOCs) available from outstanding colleges and professors. I encourage you to get involved at all these levels to continuously build your skill set and improve your adaptability. This can apply to your current job or the next one you'll be moving into at some point. Be ready.

So, in the PathForeWord there are many turns. Some you can see coming, like the road sign featured image for this entry. For others, you can't see them coming — either one of these situations needs you to be prepared by building your positive can-do outlook and your adaptable skill set through your continuous learning.

Gold Watch

I have a gold watch that was issued by a company in 1951 to a gentleman who had served for 25 years in that organization. It's been quite a change since the middle of the 20th century to the early 21st century. Neither the organization nor the individual still exist — but the gold watch exists! It exists both literally and in our imaginations of what used to be.

We feel there was an implied contract between the organization and the individual. However, I would suggest that circumstances more that commitment drove that connection. First, it was pretty tough for an individual to pick up their lives and move across the state and certainly across the nation. We think that was due in part to a greater commitment to family. But I will argue that our ability to seek out work and communicate across those miles was the chief reason for our inability to move where the pay was better and perhaps the living was better. Second, for these same reasons, the organizations of the time needed to work hard to keep their employees. It was tough to find other employees and just as tough, if not more so, to convince them to move to a new job and a new community.

Security was another one of the issues at play. You stayed close to your family because no one else would be there if you came on hard times. Today, a myriad of government agencies are available to help you during those hard times and to help you move forward. This safety net and vastly improved communication have freed us all to pursue opportunity where we find it. Likewise, it's allowed organizations to pursue the best talent, no matter where they are.

Times have indeed changed. We like to think that organizations used to look out for their employees — witness the gold watch. However, I'd point out that there were many societal and economic factors at play that drove this impression.

On my own path, I actually have a gold watch. It was issued to me when I earned my first graduate degree. It was a reward that I issued. This is the type of reward and recognition we should expect and take the time to issue on our PathForeWord. Have you received a gold watch on your path?

Nature of Work

Labor Day gives us an opportunity to further consider the nature of work. Leading up to that recent holiday Peggy Noonan penned a nice column in the Wall Street Journal titled "Work and the American Character". There were two sections that really stood out for me.

"... We talk about the financial implications of widespread high unemployment, and that isn't wrong but it misses the

central point. Joblessness is a personal crisis because work is a spiritual event."

"Work gives us purpose, stability, integration, shared mission. And so to be unable to work — unable to find or hold a job — is a kind of catastrophe for a human being."

Extending this a bit, today I attended a career focus group meeting. The guest speaker spoke about our personal identity versus the roles that we play. He noted that Europeans often get to know one another by asking, "what do you do to have fun?" Americans, on the other hand, typically ask, "what do you do?" referring almost exclusively to your job or career.

Our jobs, our careers, are a huge part of our identity, if not defining our entire sense of who we are. This brings Peggy Noonan's comments above into sharp focus — loss of job = loss of identity = personal and spiritual crisis.

I can readily relate to this sharp sense of loss and, whether I admit it or not, I'm wrestling with a personal crisis. What's next for me? Who am I (without my job)? Just what is my PathForeWord? And, why can't I see that path right now? And, perhaps without recognizing it, I'm asking to some degree, what will my identity become? What organization will I be associated with? What role will I have? In essence — who will I be?

Wow! Have we got some things up side down? Our work is important, but is it the be-all end-all of our very existence? There is, of course, Maslow's Hierarchy of Needs — something about food, shelter, and warmth. But my goodness, there has to be more to us than our jobs or careers. Yet in my own PathForeWord I've been working continuously for nearly 50 years — since starting as a bag boy in the local grocery store. In that time, I've spent countless hours either examining career paths or working on the education and training to first gain access to that

11

path and then to advance on that same path. This is the first time in all those years that I find myself unemployed. But I am not without work.

For those of you who read my blog titled My Ham Radio Adventures, you'll recall that one of my personal obsessions... er, hobbies is amateur radio. In addition, I've been able to link amateur radio to Scouting and serve in a volunteer capacity in several Radio Scouting roles. This volunteer work has made a significant difference during my time between careers. It's provided purpose and shared mission, the very things Peggy's talking about in her column. I've further established this blog and have begun to look at still other volunteer activities.

So, volunteer activities have been one way that I've been able to find some meaningful way to continue working even as I seek my next career PathForeWord. I encourage you to take some time, whether you're employed or unemployed, and examine your work-life balance, which as we've touched on above can become the very basis of your self-identity. Then seek out balance either in the work you're doing or the time you're devoting to volunteer activities, and for sure ramp up the time you're devoting to family and friends. Take some time and line up your PathForeWord.

Why Work?

I've been running through a patch of reading theological books. It all started with a biography of Dietrich Bonhoeffer. Then moved on to some of his writings and most recently to Dorothy Sayers, the great English mystery writer and apologist for the Christian faith.

In a speech delivered in England in 1942 titled "Why Work?" Dorothy Sayers makes this quite profound statement:

…Work is not, primarily, a thing one does to live, but the thing one lives to do.

She goes on to emphasize that this attitude should permeate our entire existence. A further point she makes is that with this attitude we should no longer look at work as something we get through to enjoy our leisure time, but leisure time is used primarily to recharge our batteries so that we can get back to our work — that which we live to do! She further emphasizes that with this approach we would not tolerate any limits on the number of hours or days that we steadfastly devoted to our work. Not entirely sure how this stacks up with work-life balance, but the point is that we should find work that we love.

Does this describe your attitude to your work? Something to think about long and hard as you consider your next steps on your PathForeWord.

Living Life

How does one overcome the feeling of responsibility to be at work every day? How does one learn anew the art of living life?

I'm reading Out of Africa by Isak Dinesen. Haven't yet seen the movie but really value the simple insight she provides into her life in Africa in the 1910's and 1920's. In one element of the story she describes the differences in the lives of the people of her African coffee plantation versus her European friends. She notes that in Africa the people are in unison with the time of day, phase of the moon, and seasons of the year without referring to clock or calendar

— all because they are living in the moment, mostly outdoors, and as a result, moving with the rhythms of life. She contrasts this with her visits to Europe where individuals are focused on either their study, as students, or their work as employees. They are indoors, driven to meet the next deadline, striving constantly to achieve, almost unaware of the passage of time or season.

I'm further reminded of Charles Dickens' excellent short story titled "The Child's Story". In this story, Dickens writes about the stages of life through the eyes of a child. The child recognizes from our behavior that our primary purpose in middle-age "is to always be busy."

I can certainly relate to all this. Throughout my career I've been focused not only on work but in the evenings and weekends, when not also doing extended work, I've been attending classes to advance my education and, as a result, my career. Was that summer that just passed by? Who are those other people living in my house? My children? OK, maybe it wasn't quite that bad.

Now that my career with the Boy Scouts has ended, I find as I search for the PathForeWord, I'm actually trying to return to living life as I was before. This life would include the rhythm of Monday morning, past hump day, to TGIF. It also includes the commute in the dark to start each day; to going to the car at the end of the day and recognizing that it was an awfully nice day that I'd just spent indoors tapping away on a keyboard…

How does one overcome that feeling of responsibility to be at work every day? Or overcome the need to conform to the norm of what work must inevitably look like as handed down from generation to generation? There is a different way and now is the time to find it.

As I've contemplated this key element of the PathForeWord, I've realized that I need to learn anew the art of living life. If you've got some insight into this journey, I welcome your comments and thoughts.

Risking Failure

One of the things I liked most about a recent MOOC that I attended on Design Thinking was their emphasis on taking early risks and trying quick hitting prototypes. They even said that failure was expected and valued — that's how you learned and adapted to what you'd just experienced through rapid prototyping. It further reminded me of a concept that I've grown to greatly value during my executive career — "ready, fire, aim". So often, in low risk situations, you can take several "shots" and get quite close to the target, without spending a great deal of time in analysis, review, etc.

The quote below is from one of my favorite authors —-

We pay a heavy price for our fear of failure. It is a powerful obstacle to growth. It assures the progressive narrowing of the personality and prevents exploration and experimentation. There is no learning without some difficulty and fumbling. If you want to keep on learning, you must keep on risking failure all your life. John W. Gardner

I like how he casts his perspective on growth and the requirement to explore and experiment as part of your learning process. This means failure will happen unless, as J.K. Rowling notes below you try to eliminate all risk and end up not really living.

It is impossible to live without failing at something, unless you live so cautiously that you might as well not have lived at all, in which case you have failed by default. J.K. Rowling

This isn't to say that failure is to be sought out avidly. But it does say that you must take risks in order to learn and grow. And in those risks is where you develop your skills to adapt and grow in any situation. That's the case in your job search and your career development. The PathForeWord is not always the paved road! Get out there and make something happen!

Working Through Loss

At the moment of your job loss, so many things are going through your mind, few of them positive. I recently had a first hand report from a person who was called to a conference room with 30+ people who were told to clear out their office by the end of the day. She noted that half the people in the room were crying and the other half were looking for someone to hit!

Whatever logic is behind the business decision for downsizing, outplacement, reduction-in-force, or whatever, it's almost impossible to see the good that could possibly come from it to you personally. It's going to take some time just to mourn the loss of your job, your workplace friends/family, your contribution to the business success of your organization, or even just the practice of your trade/profession. Perhaps our mourning follows the Kubler-Ross model for the stages of grief: 1) denial and isolation, just to get through that first wave of pain; 2) anger, the pain hits home; 3) bargaining, seeking to regain control; 4) depression, truly sifting through the loss; 5) acceptance, still unhappy but ready to move forward and leave this episode behind.

My friend John Clarkson characterizes at least a part of this mourning as "phantom limb syndrome". Just as when someone loses a limb, the mind still perceives the limb's presence. This can happen with your career as well. When you're separated from that previous position/career, your very identity can seem to be missing — yet linger on in your mind.

All of this says it is natural to feel deep sadness, certainly fear and concern over the future, and the pain of what amounts to rejection. It's nearly impossible to consider this a rational business decision by your former organization. How could it be rational when it causes so much pain? Yet, rational or not, it's time to face the pain and loss. There is no need to dwell on your loss. But it must be dealt with, at least over time. In that same moment, you need to be taking your next positive career steps.

On a personal note, this past weekend I phoned a dear friend of mine as he was in the midst of a surprise celebration for his retirement. He'd already had an official retirement earlier in the week. This was a weekend event his wife had organized. We couldn't make it to Nebraska, but I wanted to reach out and let him know how delighted I was to toast his success. He had just completed 40 years with his organization. It's good to note that this still happens in this day and age. But I assure you it is becoming extremely rare. Today's typical career is subject to several job losses and regrouping, retraining — whatever is needed to move forward to find your next adventure.

There is a future for you and your career. It's up to you to connect with that future. Sure you must deal with the emotional loss of your previous position, but this could be the start of an exciting new phase for your career. So leave that past position/organization behind, devoting no more energy to it than is required to help you deal with the loss, and focus all your energy on the next PathForeWord.

Job Search Framework

These are a few thoughts about what is happening in the broader employment market. This should help you put into perspective what's happening to your personal search.

Job Market

I've been thinking lately about the big changes that have occurred over the past couple of decades in the job market. Looking back to my microeconomics classes it appears to me that we have moved into a nearly perfect competition zone. This is where nearly every job is known and every applicant is readily available.

I say this because in my own career I've been able to make significant changes across industry and job type. For example, I've moved from broadcast engineer to electronics instructor to educational writer to product manager to general manager to publishing director. The associated industries ranged from television to college to manufacturer to training development and finally a nonprofit organization. Yet today I see my daughter after just five months in the workplace staying at a similar position and the exact same industry in her recent experience with a job change, with no opportunities found outside that industry. I also see similar situations with all my job-seeking colleagues — same industry, same job, or no-go.

It appears to me that this is because a company can post a job and get 100 or so applicants in the first few days if not hours, many of whom match the organization's job and industry requirements nearly perfectly. Why would they need to look across industries or job type? Why would they even consider developing talent from within when they can readily obtain the skills and experience they need from the outside?

This is a troubling assessment of the employment marketplace, at least from my perspective. I have greatly enjoyed taking on new challenges and growing into them. Some of those came about in a move from one organization to another. Others happened within the same organization as my managers recognized that I could take on other assignments to the benefit of the organization. This new marketplace, facilitated through the ready assembly and publication of information on the web, reduces the organizational need to advance employees and, as a result, it reduces an individual's prospective career horizon.

I feel a bit like Dr. Seuss's Cat in the Hat: *"And we did not like it. Not one little bit."*

In my pursuit of always looking for the PathForeWord, it occurs to me more and more that the answer is to pursue your own course outside the corporate world. It's a bit of what I'm currently doing — finding some freelance opportunities, finding some contract gigs, finding some consulting projects. I've spoken with a few people who set up their own small businesses and build their own PathForeWord. For many, I'm more and more convinced that this makes great sense. They can pick and choose their own opportunities, grow to match the ones that make sense for them, and build their own equity in their businesses. All too often a large corporation can choose to drop you based on many, many factors and you're left with your last paycheck and limited future prospects.

I'm reminded of an acquaintance who, when asked after a layoff what he did, replied that he worked for the railroad. Well that may have been his perspective but he actually did much, much more that could be of value to a prospective employer. But, he could only see that he worked for that one company. He seemed completely lost without his former company and job.

I will note that even if you've chosen to work your career through the corporate world, and many have done very well on that path, including me, it would be wise to develop your skills and experience in addition to your day job. Write a blog, take some courses, build your skill set, and even find new opportunities that you can work your way into over the course of time, or that can help with your corporate position.

Today, in what I'm describing as a job market with nearly perfect competition, you are the only one in direct charge of your PathForeWord. Make it count. Find your path — a path that you own and can grow with your own efforts.

Micro Jobs

I'm moving from my former macro-job into micro-jobs. I further see that this is a worldwide trend with many websites offering this type of hiring service for employers coupled with a job-finding/payment system for workers. It's the new economy moving at the speed of light!

Over the past few weeks I've been trying out Elance and o-Desk by setting up my profile and bidding on work. I've further been diving into the qualification tests for various types of writing assignments as well as software proficiency testing. I really like the entire system and the overall concept of bidding on work, completing assignments (I've yet to do that part, however), and receiving payment (that sounds good, too).

One recent example of how this works was a job posting for a guest blogger on career topics. This sounded great, given that I've been developing my own career oriented blog right here. So I submitted my proposal, taking care to address all that they'd asked for in their posting and providing a reasonable price for my efforts. As I submitted my proposal I noted that the job had been posted 23 hours previously, there were now 24 proposals submitted, and two interviews had already been conducted. Oh my word — talk about the new economy moving at the speed of light!

Sometimes it can get discouraging, like the example above and the intense competition. However, I really like the concept of building a portfolio of micro jobs, if you will, that can fit around your time, your interests, your skills, and give you the opportunity to pick and choose your partners. Plus, you can do this work from home. Independence like that sounds great! Now to make it happen...

While you're looking into these systems also give consideration to how you can utilize these services to get work done for your organization. In many cases there is no longer a need to hire a full- or even part-time employee when specific tasks can be farmed out to the most efficient and cost-effective individuals. For example, I saw one person who states that 90% of their work is screen capture videos including the voice-over. They've created a one-stop shop with an extremely narrow service offering, but one that has to be very cost-effective, lightning quick, with excellent results. There are many similar examples.

I encourage you to check out micro jobs from both the employee and employer perspective. It is the PathForeWord in the new light speed economy.

Strength = Juice

Check out the book and video series called "Go Put Your Strengths to Work" by Marcus Buckingham. I'm watching the video series with a group of twenty or so. It is a career transition group called Mag!c, which stands for Marketing, Advertising, Graphics, and Communications. Of course there would be an exclamation mark in there somewhere!

The group is very supportive, encouraging, and helpful as we are all in transition to the next stage of our careers. Plus, since it is composed of marketing types, we share some common experiences and background. It is also great fun to celebrate when someone finds that next stage in his or her career. It also helps us recognize that people do end this transition phase at some point.

The Strengths video series has been very enlightening. It moves on from the StrengthsFinders series into not necessarily what you do best but what gives you the most "juice" in your work. What that means is — what is it that gets you into the "flow" of work? This is when you start on something and the next time you look up several hours have passed. You're engaged in the task that is a natural part of your being. The emphasis in the video is to find those strengths and start playing to them — and do it right now!

My favorite quote is that after working a great deal on one of his weaknesses Marcus reports that he "went from terrible to really bad". He also notes that you may be very good at math and let's say accounting. Yet after just a few hours working on those tasks you're completely drained. It clearly doesn't give you "juice". The trick is to find those tasks that essentially harmonize with your spirit.

One of his stories is about how he stuttered as a youth. Yet, whenever volunteers were sought out for a public speaking assignment, his hand went up. He noted one speaking

22

assignment in elementary school with 400 students in the audience. His practice was terrible, but when he got up in front of the audience, it went perfectly. Something inside him drove him to those tasks to harmonize with his strengths and desires.

It's good stuff. Be sure to include this book and video series on your PathForeWord and start identifying and using those strengths!

Networking

The most important part of your job search will be networking. People hire people they know of who others that they know recommend. Get out and start connecting with all those you've worked with and whom you come into contact with through job search focus groups, industry associations, etc. Then never ever stop networking even after you've found your next stop on your PathForeWord.

Making Connections

You can read the stats and listen to the testimonials. From those it's clear that you find jobs and other opportunities through your connections. So the logic is to build your network of connections. In today's digital world, those connections can be readily facilitated through LinkedIn. Even so, how do you really find those connections? How do you make them work for your job search?

In order to make connections work you need to have a targeted plan for your job campaign. What job or position are you seeking? In what industry? What targeted companies? Once these key questions have been answered as part of your thoughts and planning, it becomes a great deal easier to determine who to contact and what help you need to make the desired connections.

Note, too, that this is clearly a two-way connection street that you're traveling. When working with your network, always include the statement "how can I help you?" This is particularly true as you build that network across job search focus groups or career transition workshops or better yet at industry association meetings.

For me in my early PathForeWord, I've not yet targeted companies or even positions; I've got the "go slow" part down well. However, I've learned how to help others and through that process how to network. For example, I've recently connected with an engineer who is finding the boom and bust cycle of the defense business to be less than desirable. He's thinking about law school and leveraging his technical skill into working in the intellectual property field. Well, I have a great connection who is already working is this area, not as an attorney but as an engineer. So the possibility for this engineer is to start now in that field. To help in that potential process, I've reached out to my contact and cleared the way for the two to get together for an exploratory phone call to learn more about the field of interest. Will it lead to a job? Not likely, but it will provide further information about the considered PathForeWord and perhaps a boost in the right direction.

Was this connection a benefit to my job search? Perhaps, as the engineer does have contacts in the corporate communication field. But the real benefit to me was helping someone else in their PathForeWord and gaining first hand experience into how this connection process works. This, in turn, helps me better understand what I'm asking someone else to do on my behalf to facilitate the connection that I'm seeking.

So my suggestion is to get out there and start making connections. Ask the question "how can I help you?" and see where it leads in your own PathForeWord.

Support Networks

In my PathForeWord I've relied on an extensive network of friends, colleagues, and family to support me over the years. Plus, I've generally invested time and effort to support them. But this vital network of support really comes to the forefront when you're in a crunch, such as looking for your next adventure. On my current path, I've reached out to a large number of people to learn and engage. Doing my best along the way to offer my own insight and support to their efforts.

Around my recent work at the National Scout Jamboree, I came across some exceptional examples of support. First, our 40+ volunteer staff members stepped up to make some great things happen for the Scouts. Then, following the Jamboree, two members stepped forward to offer to transport and store all the gear in preparation for the next Jamboree. These were the same guys that poured their heart into making key contributions to the operation and then stepped further forward to help for the long run. What a joy it is to work with them and what a remarkable contribution they make in supporting our operation and supporting me in my leadership role.

Yet another true friend took steps toward the end of the Jamboree to get me up into a helicopter to tour the facilities. Then, for the evening after the Jamboree closed, set me up in a local resort where key donors and guests had been staying during the Jamboree. He was really looking after me and thereby provided my first hot shower, great meal, and real bed since I arrived at the Jamboree fifteen days before! Not only did he do all this, but also provided a recommendation of my work to a prospective employer that has so far resulted in a phone interview with the hiring manager. What a true friend and what great support to me and my efforts.

I trust that in your own PathForeWord you've had key people step up and really help you out. As you can see from the short snapshot above, I've had lots of great people support me over the years. But I do find that I need to find more ways to exhibit this support to those in my network. It truly, truly needs to be a two-way PathForeWord. How are you doing on your two-way path?

Ups and Downs

I recently experienced my first phone interview in my current career adventure. As soon as I learned the date and time I began my research on the hiring manager (unknown to me until that moment) and then a fair bit of study on interviewing. On the latter, I'd studied and worked all the other areas of the job search on the outplacement firm's website and in various workshops. But, I hadn't even begun to explore the interviewing topics. Of course, I'd spent a fair bit of time over the last several years on the other side of the hiring process and spent considerable time studying interviewing. But it has always been critical for me to prepare well for the interview, particularly in getting ready to tell my career success stories. Those stories are not always top of mind. Plus, I want to be sure of my facts. So, study is an important part of preparing for the interview.

While studying both the organization, the hiring manager, more details about the position, and my own success stories, I became really, really excited about the opportunity. In fact, my mind considered that an in-person interview would only be a few days away and I'd be on the job perhaps a couple of weeks away at the most! At the close of the phone interview, which went well, I learned that many more candidate reviews were ahead and that the process was at a very early stage. Once those thoughts entered my mind, it became a downhill slide, doubting that anything would move forward, at least for me.

So, the PathForeWord not only has twists and turns even losses, it also has a fair bit of ups and downs. In this case all the ups and downs were in my own emotional state as I

27

considered the current event and the likely outcomes. This is something to consider in your own PathForeWord. I'll also note that the very next day I was more upbeat about the potential for this position. I believe it is called irrepressible spirit! It is something we should all take steps to develop and nurture in ourselves and in those around us.

Good Turn

Having spent a considerable part of my career, not to mention my youth, involved with the Boy Scouts, you can well imagine that "doing a good turn daily" is never very far from my thoughts. In my current PathForeWord I'm engaged with a number of networking groups, working together to help connect each other to our next career adventure. All those groups use the phrase "Help One Person Everyday" which is represented by the acronym H.O.P.E. Of course, doing a good turn and helping one person everyday are essentially the same thing.

At this point in my PathForeWord I've generally settled on seeking out freelance writing assignments and beginning to do so through online marketplaces like Elance and oDesk as well as contract agencies. While most of the discussion at career networking groups is around finding full-time positions, which isn't quite what I'm focusing on, I've gone into the last several meetings with the express primary purpose of helping others. This chiefly involves helping others identify resources that can assist their job search or to connect them to people in my own network that can provide perspective on organizations or provide insight into industry segments or career fields.

Along this path I'm finding many people who are really paying it forward. Most recently I've found an individual who is providing a free four Saturday course in preparation for the Project Management Professional examination. I've also found a career coach who is providing free coaching on using the StrengthsFinders results in your job search. He is also providing workshops on the new landscape for careers based on the growing pace of creative destruction of entire industries. With the latter, I've offered to help with improved marketing strategy and communication to extend the reach of the courses. We'll see how that goes.

All of this serves several purposes. First, it gets us engaged with others and making a difference in their lives. Second, it shifts the focus from ourselves and our own paths. And, third, it activates our thinking around networking and provides a reason to reach out to many others in our own networks.

Bottom line, what are you doing in your PathForeWord to Help One Person Everyday, or to do a Good Turn Daily?

Age Bias

Over the years I've seen a fair bit of age bias. It can take subtle forms --- I recall the phrase, "you're over-qualified for the position." Most people have decided to discard that phrasing. Now they just say you don't meet the requirements.

That particular phrase has always seemed oxymoronic, at least to me. I always, always sought out the over-qualified candidate to fill open positions. Admittedly, it took more of my time to work with this level of staff member. Leadership meant more consultation and agreement over action steps, when that was required. More often than not, no discussion was needed since the over-qualified employee understood the organizational goals and could make better decisions based on their experience and qualifications. It made my job easy and I had a team of highly skilled staff members that could really drive the organization forward.

I have also heard the phrase, "I want some eager 20-something to take on this assignment." They usually note that they can also better afford the salary for that younger person. See the above paragraph for one of my opinions on this approach. As to salary, economics tells us that there is a market rate for the specific job that needs to be filled. That doesn't vary by the level of qualifications/experience that any particular person brings to the job. Many, many highly qualified and experienced professionals would be glad to take on lower level positions.

Indeed, another topic of discussion along these lines is the typical trajectory of a career path. It doesn't always go up. We may not even want it to go up. As you gain experience as a manager, there comes a time when you no longer want to supervise lots of people. You're ready to step back and make an individual contribution. But while the employee may be ready for this type of change, the organization often isn't. This, of course, would require a step back in compensation as well. Somehow we all need to get our brains around this approach to a career --- enabling employees to continue to make a contribution but at a lower level, perhaps even part-time level.

On this line of thought, I've fairly recently spent some time with job search focus groups populated by "seasoned" professionals. I was startled by the incredibly talented and experienced people present who were struggling to find their next career adventure. Now, it was also true that some of those "seasoned" professionals were not over-qualified at all. In fact, I've often quipped that some had one-year of experience repeated twenty times, rather than twenty-years of experience growing and improving their performance. Plus, they had often let their training and certifications slip over time. That's something for another blog post. Yet there are many who have continued to grow and improve their performance, including building certifications and training along the way, who are still struggling to find that next career adventure, based in large part on age bias.

A friend of mine provided me with this wonderful comment ---

"Age is a marker of time, not spirit." Marta Stiglin, Stiglin Consulting

She was responded to my note to her about attending a two-week training camp with about 90% twenty-somethings and attempting to fit in and contribute. In that particular circumstance, my fellow classmates actually seemed to adopt me and overly encourage me through the class. It felt great and I learned so much. But the comment stands --- it's about your spirit, not your age --- or at least it should be.

So, what to do in your job search or in mapping out your career path given this inherent bias? Here's a brief list of thoughts along those lines:

- **Appearance** --- No comb overs, get new glasses, look at your wardrobe. Today's male style of short haircuts can really benefit us balding guys. Try the health club and get fit.

- **LinkedIn/Resume** --- Drop the dates on your degrees, drop the first 10-20 years of your experience, emphasize your recent experience and training. Unfortunately, the accomplishments based resume doesn't really work any more, but you can customize your resume for each job posting.

- **Presence** --- Smile, engage those you meet, actively participate in the workplace, join special teams and initiatives.

- **Adjust Your Price** --- Basic economics tells us that price is about value provided to the organization. Adjust your expectations around the value of the work that you can deliver given the job you can secure.

- **Organization** --- Find an organization that supports old folks! Either that or start your own.

That's my brief list. Give this some of your considered thought. Let me know what I've missed via the comments field below. Finally, get ready for this phase of your career. No matter your age, age bias will find you. Your job is to first overcome it and second to take advantage of other employers' blind spot and recruit some of the best talent available for your organization.

Resume Tips

I've recently attended several workshops and sought advice from many around developing a resume. I'm sure that I haven't yet completed that exercise as I'll always be seeking ways of improving the presentation and, in particular, customizing each resume for the specific job — always trying to connect with the hiring manager after getting through the hurdles of machine sorting and recruiter vetting. Here's my journey and what I've learned so far in this particular PathForeWord.

Resume Evolution

Below I've provided some images showing at a glance the evolution of my resume so far. The beginning image is the long form resume that I originally developed some years ago. It covers my work history in-depth and runs up to five pages. The next image is the resume that emerged from my work with an outplacement firm. I used one of their online tools to craft my very first accomplishments or functional based resume. I was quite pleased with this effort and was roundly congratulated on my work by the outplacement firm.

Jim Wilson

2605 Valleywood Drive
Grapevine, TX 76051

Office: (972) 580-2010
Home: (817) 571-4260
E-mail: jim@k5nd.us

Executive Profile

Senior Executive with combined technical, educational, and multimedia publishing expertise and proven success in project management, product management, P&L management, staff training/development, marketing, finance, and customer satisfaction. Consistently achieved organizational performance improvement through the application of technology and employee empowerment to streamline production processes and improve customer service. Extensive experience in organizational transition, division mergers, team building, and working with highly creative people to achieve organizational goals.

Results-oriented leader able to assess situations, establish goals/objectives, and implement action plans to achieve those goals and objectives.

- 75% reduction in management layers and overall payroll savings of 40% through two-division consolidation.
- 83% reduction in production process time while reducing errors through application of TQM methods.
- $3 million annual savings through merging departments, introducing technology, improving productivity.
- Increased billable time by 100%. Improved customer satisfaction by 40%+.
- Selected and implemented Content Management System for organization web sites.

Project Management	Team Building
Product Management	Customer Satisfaction
Technical Training Development	P & L Management
Educational Product Development	Division Mergers
Magazine and Book Publishing	Streamline Processes and Structure

Professional Experience

Boy Scouts of America, National Headquarters, Irving, TX   1992 to Present
Director, Media Services & Public Relations, 2008 to present.
- Responsible for all media production through the 20+ employee Media Studio, includes all print, web, video production with all editorial, graphic design, production, and over 100 contractors from freelance authors to illustrators, and subject matter experts in topics from camping to nuclear energy.
- Responsible for public relations, internal communication, and the Boy Scout of America 100th Anniversary project office.
- Responsible for National Scout Museum operations

In August 2008 after major reorganization of the National Headquarters, organized a new department within a consolidated marketing organization. Recruited a key manager for the Media Studio, implemented streamlined production processes, established internal communication management position, and consolidated public relations under a single manager.

Jim Wilson

Communicator | Organizer | Builder

jbwilson@me.com
http://www.linkedin.com/in/jbwilson
http://www.PathForeWord.com

2605 Valleywood Drive
Grapevine, TX 76051
682-217-4030

Summary

Communicator: written and spoken word, focused on getting your message out—activating audiences. Organizer: teams and projects, bringing order from chaos, getting things done effectively, efficiently. Builder: products and people, tireless focus on continuous improvement in all areas.

Action-oriented leader in marketing communications, creative services, and technical/educational publishing in all media formats. Proven success in program development, event leadership, strategic change, project management, and product management. Implemented strategic organizational change, division and department mergers. Experience in both for-profit and non-profit organizations. Excellent writer from technical training to executive speeches. Seeking assignments that can have a direct impact on your organization. Driven by mission.

Selected Accomplishments

Program Development—Established and recruited the first National Radio Scouting Committee. Directed their volunteer efforts to build an extensive website with support materials for Scout Councils and amateur radio operators. Built and implemented an intensive promotion campaign to both audiences, developed supporting relationship with national amateur radio association, sought out and established sponsorship relationships with industry manufacturers for Jamboree and Jamboree on the Air support. Grew USA Scout Jamboree on the Air participation in 2011 by 600% and again in 2012 by 480% (454 in 2010 to 3,185 in 2011 and 18,537 in 2012). Boy Scouts of America.

Event Leadership—National Scout Jamboree 2010, fulfilled top leadership role for the Jamboree Media Center staffed by 150 volunteers producing a daily newspaper, 24/7 radio broadcast, Home Town News for Scout reporters, leaders' newsletter and website, media relations, crisis communication, photography, and websites. National Scout Jamboree 2013, direct leadership for 45 volunteers running the K2BSA amateur radio demonstration station, Radio Merit Badge training, amateur radio direction finding course, and contact with the International Space Station. Provided amateur radio demonstrations for over 2,600 Scouts, with 340 earning the Radio Merit Badge. Boy Scouts of America.

Strategic Change—Implemented significant strategic shift in internal publishing department adding advertising agency skill sets and projects to existing base of technical publishing. Hired creative director, ramped up account management skills, installed new project management and billing system. Internal client partnership effectiveness survey showed 39 out of 82 responses rating at 9 and above on a 10-point scale. Significant improvement in appearance and brand compliance for 1,200 projects each year. Boy Scouts of America.

Department Merger—Merged three operations into single internal publishing/communication division, implemented publishing technology, reduced staff 14%, increased billable time 100%, achieved in excess of $2 million savings. Implemented customer satisfaction measures and moved from 69% to 90% in two years, followed by steady improvement to 97% four years later, remaining in the high 90% range for the next several years. Boy Scouts of America.

1

35

The next image, below, retains the accomplishment/functional format but moves into bullet points. This came about based on feedback at the Southlake Career Transition Workshop. You can see that it is much easier to read and a great deal more inviting to read rather than the text heavy previous version.

Jim Wilson   Communicator | Organizer | Builder

jbwilson@me.com
http://www.linkedin.com/in/jbwilson
http://www.PathForeWord.com

2605 Valleywood Drive
Grapevine, TX 76051
682-217-4030 mobile

Publishing and Communication Executive

Communicator: written and spoken word, focused on getting your message out—activating audiences.
Organizer: teams and projects, bringing order from chaos, getting things done effectively, efficiently.
Builder: organizations and people, tireless focus on continuous improvement in all areas.

Experienced in technical/educational publishing, creative services, and communications in all media formats. Deep experience in non-profit organizations. Excellent writer from technical training to executive speeches. Seeking assignments with direct impact on your organization. Driven by mission.

Selected Accomplishments

Strategic Change
- Implemented significant strategic change in internal publishing department adding advertising agency skill sets and projects to existing base of technical publishing.
- Built, with all staff members, new department charter with purpose, mission, goals, and measures.
- Introduced Teamwork 10 commandments to guide daily operational approach.
- Hired creative director. Ramped up client-focused account management skills.
- Installed new project management and billing system.
- Internal client partnership effectiveness survey showed 39 out of 82 responses rating at 9 and above on a 10-point scale after first year.

Project Management
- Led team of 40 staff members to revise 119 merit badge pamphlets from one-color to four-color.
- Revised 9,500 pages, 11,000 images/photos, 1.4 million books printed.
- Total project cost $1.5 million, completed on time over a twelve-month time frame.
- Accomplished amidst the normal production workload of 1,500 projects annually.

Department Merger
- Merged three operations into single internal publishing/communication division.
- Implemented publishing technology, reduced staff 14%, increased billable time 100%, achieved in excess of $2 million annual savings.
- Implemented customer satisfaction measures and moved from 69% to 90% in two years, followed by steady improvement to 97% four years later.

Cost Savings
- Downsized from 50 to 24 staff members. Based staffing on previous labor billing across categories.
- Built minimum level operation to best meet internal client needs.
- Tapped contract labor to fill gaps and meet seasonal demand.
- Added public relations, internal communications, 100th anniversary project, and National Scouting Museum to direct reports.

The next version, and final for this slide show but by no means final effort, is the result of attending the day-long Frisco Career Transition Workshop. Here's their workbook's comment about resume format —

The chronological format is king. If your resume is on the job boards in a functional format, it is equivalent to having the steering wheel of a car on the right side… in the back seat.

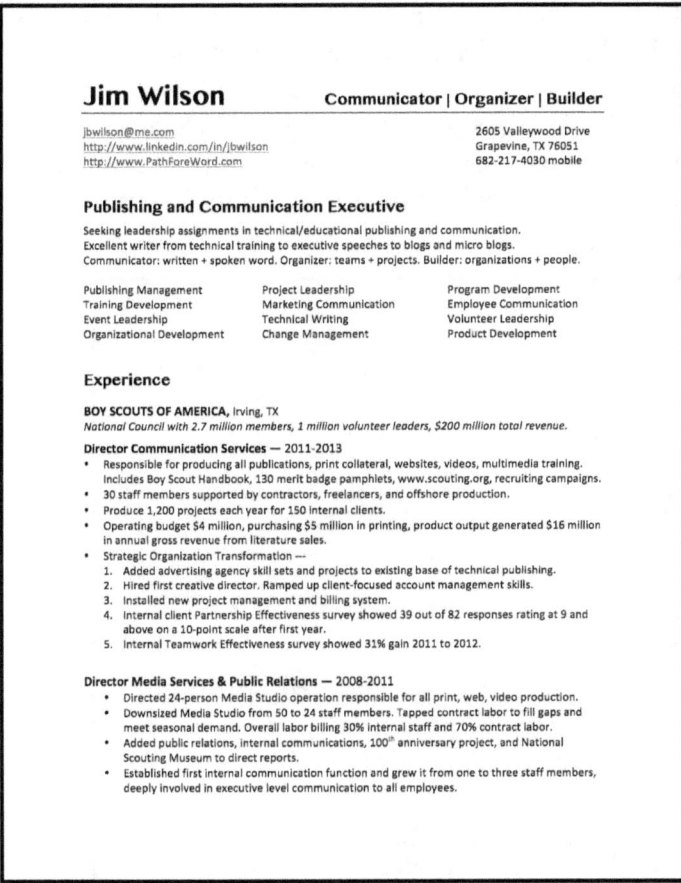

The reason for some of this formatting is to get through the machine scanners and to the recruiter.

Your Six-Second Casting Call

Once with the recruiter, if you're fortunate enough to get your resume in front of the recruiter, they will be spending roughly six seconds with each resume. Oh my goodness! It doesn't sound like much time does it? All of which means you need to better understand how to reach that recruiter with your message. The folks at the Frisco Career Transition Workshop shared some "gaze trace analysis" on where the recruiter spends their time with the resume. I've attempted to provide a limited glimpse into that research below.

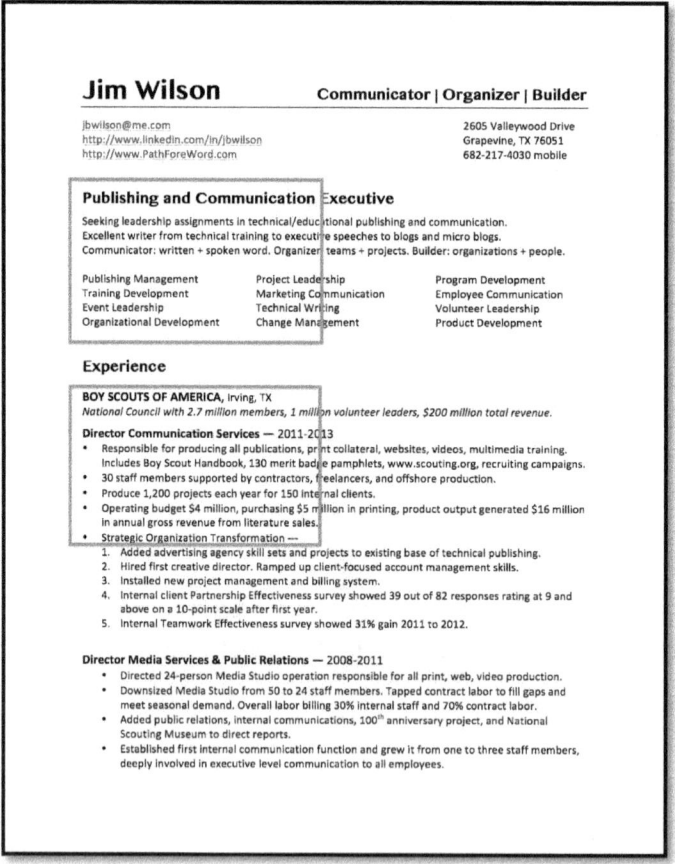

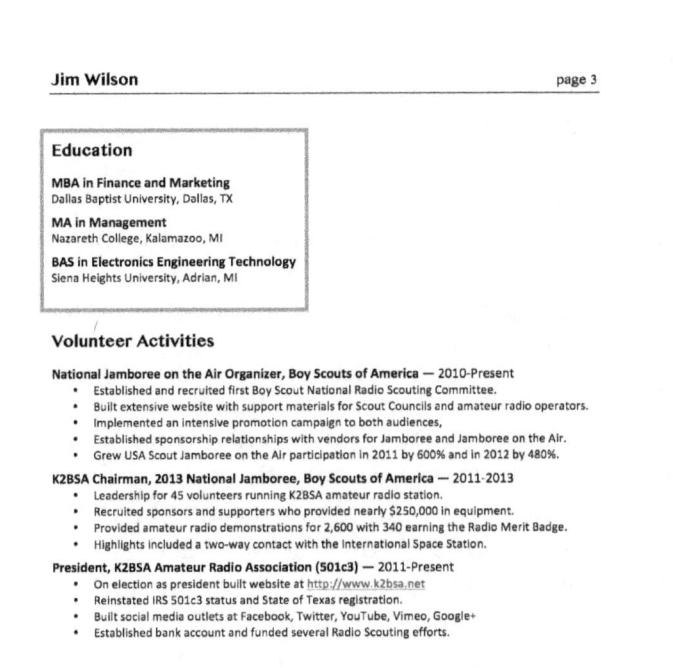

Education

MBA in Finance and Marketing
Dallas Baptist University, Dallas, TX

MA in Management
Nazareth College, Kalamazoo, MI

BAS in Electronics Engineering Technology
Siena Heights University, Adrian, MI

Volunteer Activities

National Jamboree on the Air Organizer, Boy Scouts of America — 2010-Present
- Established and recruited first Boy Scout National Radio Scouting Committee.
- Built extensive website with support materials for Scout Councils and amateur radio operators.
- Implemented an intensive promotion campaign to both audiences,
- Established sponsorship relationships with vendors for Jamboree and Jamboree on the Air.
- Grew USA Scout Jamboree on the Air participation in 2011 by 600% and in 2012 by 480%.

K2BSA Chairman, 2013 National Jamboree, Boy Scouts of America — 2011-2013
- Leadership for 45 volunteers running K2BSA amateur radio station.
- Recruited sponsors and supporters who provided nearly $250,000 in equipment.
- Provided amateur radio demonstrations for 2,600 with 340 earning the Radio Merit Badge.
- Highlights included a two-way contact with the International Space Station.

President, K2BSA Amateur Radio Association (501c3) — 2011-Present
- On election as president built website at http://www.k2bsa.net
- Reinstated IRS 501c3 status and State of Texas registration.
- Built social media outlets at Facebook, Twitter, YouTube, Vimeo, Google+
- Established bank account and funded several Radio Scouting efforts.

I've placed boxes over the three places they felt were the most critical. The top of the resume looking at your objective/summary, the most recent chronological position, and on education, typically at the bottom of the final page of the resume. There were a few other key items in their research, mostly around recent positions, but these seem to me like the big ones. They essentially identify the key real estate on your resume.

Pin-Point Focus

Given all this feedback, I was beginning to reel from all the information, sometimes conflicting. At that point one of my fellow job seekers offered to provide her perspective. She's an HR Director with considerable experience reviewing resumes and making hiring recommendations and decisions. Her first criteria for our coaching session was to bring along a job posting as well as the resume that I'd forward for that job. So, she was bringing the resume review into the true context of the job search.

She first went through the job posting, highlighting all the key items for that position. She then noted that first the title of the resume needs to reflect the title of the position. Then, all key words and accomplishments need to be focused on the key items for that position. The other accomplishments, though of considerable interest to you, are really not of interest to the recruiter. After all, they have only six seconds to place your resume in the stack for further consideration!

This might be tough medicine to swallow for most of us. But, it is right on the mark. The hallmark of any worthwhile communication program is its laser focus on the audience. With your resume, the audience is first the scanning machine and software, then the recruiter, and finally the hiring manager. All three are looking for key words and matching accomplishments. Of further keen interest is that the first two in this sequence have a list of the key words but don't necessarily know their meaning. Nor would they be able to pick out otherwise applicable experience from your resume. This means you have to hit those same keywords or get tossed. The good news — the key words are in their job description.

This topic could well continue into all sorts of areas within the resume itself and particularly into cover letters. However, this is just a brief intro into this important career topic. You'll need to seek out more detailed career insight from those experts who are much closer to this topic. I recommend you try out your local transition workshops and job networking groups. From there you can find connections that can give your personal attention and help you better understand what you need to do to connect with your next career adventure.

From all this you can see that my own PathForeWord will involve even more wholesale modification of my basic resume along with laser focus revisions for each position. I wish you well in your own journey and hope this has helped.

LinkedIn

In my PathForeWord writing business I've started to take on some clients who have asked me to write their resumes, cover letters, and update their LinkedIn profiles. They are savvy enough to realize that you need not only a specific cover letter for each job application but also a customized resume to highlight the skills and experience you can bring to that specific job. You may recall that I've been suggesting this approach since my passage through resume purgatory.

They have also started to see recruiters visit their LinkedIn profiles. This often happens right after they forward their resume and cover letter. The good news is that their resume and cover letter are making an impact with recruiters. The even better news is that they have yet another opportunity to impress that recruiter with their polished LinkedIn profile. Before we get into profiles, let's look more closely at the world of LinkedIn that currently holds 300 million profiles.

Social Network

When I first started to explore social media, many years ago, the first one I could really connect with was LinkedIn. I immediately understood the benefit of connecting with fellow professionals. Moreover, I loved the search function where I could really narrow the search focus. I actually found a number of former colleagues and was able to catch up with them. Thus began the process of building my LinkedIn network. This is one of the key features of LinkedIn. Take those business cards you've been collecting and start building your LinkedIn network. Remember that great boss? Find her and connect.

The job search recommendation is to build your network to at least 500. This is where the connection counter on your profile will top out. It will read 500+. This number will help you show up in recruiter searches. It will also help you find links to people you'd like to contact to learn more about any company that you're trying to penetrate.

One of my job search experiences was trying to learn more about a small non-profit. I could find just two people on LinkedIn that had this organization on their profiles. For one of them, I found a direct connection of mine who I had met in a job search focus group. I reached out to him, he forwarded my request and while I didn't make that connection, I did get a response from the recruiter! I learned later that they were told to forward all such requests to the recruiter for follow up. So, a web of connections helped me make the critical connection I was seeking. Bottom line, relentlessly build your network on LinkedIn.

Professional Groups

The next level of connection is through LinkedIn Groups. There are all manner of groups that have been established on LinkedIn. They can be groups that exist outside of LinkedIn, such as professional organizations. They can be groups that exist only on LinkedIn, such as discussion groups around a particular topic. The job search recommendation is that you join at least 50 groups. You should also select a few and become active in the discussions. All this gets your profile showing up in recruiter searches. It is also helpful when you want to make a connection outside your range of first level contacts. If you share a group with the person you're trying to contact, that is a perfect way to open the connection. Moreover, LinkedIn allows you to make that invitation to connect directly since you're in the same group.

Company Pages

There are also company pages on LinkedIn. In fact, any time someone enters a company on their profile it links to that company page. I've created one for PathForeWord. For your job search the big benefit is that you can follow companies of interest. In addition, they will often post jobs on LinkedIn. Plus, they help you find connections within the company for your further research and contact.

Job Postings

Another huge benefit of LinkedIn is their job opening postings. You can search these openings based on your key words. You can save those searches and run them on a scheduled basis. LinkedIn will also alert you to openings that match your search criteria. Furthermore, some job postings actually identify the recruiter that posted the job. So you can reach out to promote your candidacy for the position.

Individual Profiles

Perhaps the biggest advantage of LinkedIn is publishing your own information via your profile. As noted above there are now 300 million users on LinkedIn. So you can imagine that a few best practices have been determined. That will be the subject of my next post --- how to optimize your LinkedIn profile. This will be a great next stop on your PathForeWord. See you then.

You Are Who You Appear to Be

"You are who you appear to be." I'm quoting the guy that hired me to take on massive challenges at a training development operation. At first I was stunned. Shouldn't people look beyond appearances to find the "real" person? Isn't there more to who we are than our appearance?

Perhaps. But in the lightning world of recruiting and hiring, people don't have time, or better said, don't take the time to move beyond appearances. You'll recall the research work that revealed that recruiters spend six-seconds reviewing your resume. I call it "your six-second casting call."

So appearances are important. While you can address that requirement with your superbly crafted cover letter and resume, both targeted at the specific position and organization you're pursuing, it is often your LinkedIn profile that will be used as follow-on information by recruiters. It is also your LinkedIn profile that will be searched by recruiters, and others, looking to fill important positions which you haven't even heard about.

Profile Editing

So let's get down to editing that all important LinkedIn Profile. The first thing to do is select "Edit Profile." At the right hand side of the page where it says "Notify Your Network" select "No." Otherwise, every change will be broadcast to your network of connections --- the 500+ list of contacts that you are growing. Which, in turn, will lead to people congratulating you on your new position titled "Seeking my next career adventure." Which loosely translated means "I'm unemployed" or "I'm looking to move to a new job." When you've completed this round of editing, change the setting to broadcast changes to your connections. Then make one more change to alert them that your profile has been updated.

Profile Settings

This is also a good time to look over your profile privacy settings. You can find this by mousing over the photo in the upper right hand of the page and selecting "Privacy and Settings." The only thing I would note here is that you should turn off your activity broadcasts while you're editing your profile, as noted above. Also under "select what others see when you view their profile" I would opt for "your name and headline." Otherwise you will not be able to see who has viewed your profile. This is something that you'll want to monitor as you apply for positions. Often times after you've applied for a position you can actually see that the recruiter has viewed your profile. Then you have another connection to pursue.

Profile Photo

At the top of your LinkedIn profile is your photo. Since this is a professional networking site, your photo should also be professional. Try not to match your Facebook photo. You know the one where you cropped out the other people in the photo just to capture your own head shot. Too bad about the arm that is wrapped around your shoulder in that photo.

Take the time to capture a professional photo. You don't have to schedule a sitting with a professional photographer. One of our local social media experts tells the story of giving his wife his cellphone and having her take literally hundreds of photos of him while moving around the house and posing with different expressions. Out of that, he captured just the right look for his dynamic LinkedIn profile. My own photo was taken at a business conference where a vendor set up portrait lighting along with a professional photographer and offered free profile photos in exchange for your contact information.

One further note on your profile photo --- use your keywords in your file name. I was amazed to hear about this search optimization technique at a workshop. It makes sense. You want your name and your keywords everywhere. Your profile photo filename is one more opportunity to turn recruiter searches in your direction.

Public Profile URL

Make sure you've updated your LinkedIn Public Profile URL with a strong username. When you first set up your account, LinkedIn assigned your profile a number. You can edit that by clicking on "Edit" near the URL information directly under your profile photo. I've been able to select jbwilson for my user name. It will tell you if your selection is available when you attempt to edit it. Once you have a more user-friendly profile URL, you can add it to your resume, business cards, etc.

Contact Information

Next to the URL is the button to edit your contact information. I've elected to include all my contact information including phone number, email address, and physical address. You can also provide links to your Twitter account and any websites, such as your blog. I also include this contact information in the profile Summary. You want to take every opportunity to help the recruiter make contact with you about that next career adventure.

Compelling Headline

Well, we've spent a great deal of time on some details. Now we get into the content of your profile. But first a word from our sponsor --- branding.

"You are who you appear to be." And so much of who you appear to be is about your personal branding. If you haven't already starting thinking this way while preparing your resume and cover letters, now is a good time to start. Everything that is posted on this profile is about your personal brand. That branding work must start with your compelling headline. You've only got so many words to use in this space. I've chosen to use my personal branding statement "Freelance Writer | Consultant | Blogger." I use this same statement on my resume, website, business cards, etc. It also helps with my one-minute (or is it 30-second?) elevator speech. Work on that headline until you find one that really fits your personal brand. [This is my second brand statement. The first was Communicator | Organizer | Builder. This fit my early goal of obtaining a director level position. Now I'm focused on my freelance and consulting business.]

Next in this section is your Location and Industry. I've selected the broader geographical location --- the Dallas/Fort Worth area --- as recruiters can better relate to this over my hometown of Grapevine, which could be in any part of Texas for all they know. For me, selecting an industry was challenging as my career has including publishing, communication, writing, etc. Pick the broadest category that best fits your career goals.

Action-Packed Summary

If the Summary section isn't shown on your profile, add it from the list which should be at the right of your profile. This is a completely open block of text that you can use to really sell your skills and demonstrate how you can solve problems for potential employers. This is also where you can list your keywords. Finally, I've also used it to provide my contact information. I suggest searching through other LinkedIn profiles in your industry to see examples of how people are sharing their personal message and, yes, branding, on their summary. Then using those examples as inspiration, draft your own that sell your skills and experience to potential employers.

Note that you can also add links or upload files to your Summary, as well as all the other content blocks on LinkedIn. I've chosen to provide a link to my visual resume on YouTube and to provide a PDF file of my executive biography.

Experience

The next item on your profile should be Experience. Note that you can move these items around by grabbing the up/down arrow on the far right and dragging that section up or down on your profile. This applies to all the major categories as well as the individual items, such as positions within your experience. I suggest leading with your Summary, followed by Experience. However, if you're a recent college graduate, you may want to lead with your Education.

Next add your positions, with dates of employment, company, etc. to your experience. Here you can take a bit more time providing details about your accomplishments in each position versus what you can do on a resume. You can also add links and files to each of the positions. On some of mine, I've chosen to add reports or presentations. In looking at this again, I should probably add one or more videos. This is an opportunity to show off your best work. This is something you can't readily do on a resume or cover letter.

On my profile I've elected to show most of my executive positions but not my early days in the Air Force and other early technical jobs. Even at that, I'm showing far more than I typically would on a targeted resume. Some of that is due to the fact that I'm trying to make as many connections as possible. Part of it is because I'm proud of those achievements and want to show them off. You may elect to narrow what you present. As a writer, I'm trained to be concise and to the point. But sometimes I just can't help myself...

Education

My big recommendation around Education is to not show the dates unless you have a compelling reason to do so. Even though my education is relatively recent, having earned my degrees well after I started my career, it is still so last century. There is no need to date yourself and have a recruiter consciously or unconsciously rule you out before you've even been considered.

Skills and Endorsements

The Skills and Endorsements section lists those skills where someone else on LinkedIn has endorsed you. It can become quite a long list. Your choices here are whether to display them and where to display them in your profile. You can also elect to add or delete skills. You have an overall limit of showing 50.

Recommendations

LinkedIn also allows written recommendations that can be displayed on your profile. These are directly associated with positions shown on your profile. I have recommendations for nearly every position. I've always thought that this is one of the more powerful features of LinkedIn. I will note, however, that I've been called numerous times for reference checks, often on those for whom I've written LinkedIn recommendations. In those calls, the recruiters seem to be unaware of my written recommendations. So I'm not sure that it is as effective as I'd like to believe.

Even so, I recommend that you ask some of your key connections to provide written recommendations. They only need to be a few words. Plus, you can either suggest to them a few keywords that they should use in your recommendation or even provide them some language that they can use, modify, or discard. This is something for you to consider as you're building your profile. I feel this is a really cool feature of LinkedIn.

Volunteer Experiences and Causes

Another category of information that you can add to your profile is "Volunteer Experiences and Causes." If you don't have much going on in this space, there is no need to display it on your profile. On my profile, I have a great deal of experience in this area. Plus, much of that experience can directly apply to potential positions and assignments. So I've played it up quite extensively.

Other Categories

There are a number of other categories of information that you can add to your profile. For example, Groups that you belong to can be sorted and selected to be visible on your profile or not. I've added an extensive listing of Publications to my profile, since that's a big part of what I do. However, I have not listed Patents, since I don't have any. You may want to list Courses of special note for your professional or personal development. Projects could also be an interesting category to add. I may do that as I complete some of my current consulting assignments. I have used Test Scores to highlight my StrengthsFinders top five strengths. So this gives you get an idea of how to use some of these categories to enhance your overall presentation on this important platform.

"You are who you appear to be"

This phrase is so apt when it comes to your LinkedIn profile. Spend some time now and return often to update your profile. If you're not currently engaged in the job search process, you will be at some point in the future. So take the time right now to start building your profile as well as establishing and refining your personal brand. Furthermore, don't be afraid to change your personal branding and presentation. You're always gaining new insight and developing your perspective on who you really are and/or want to become. LinkedIn is a great way to get that down in writing and try it out.

This process is one that never stops, just as your personal development never stops. It is all part of your PathForeWord. Good luck.

Cover Letters

Recently I was working with a friend on a cover letter. I forwarded several examples and provided a fair bit of information on what I'd learned during workshops as well as during meetings over coffee with recruiting experts. Then I realized that I hadn't yet shared that information on my career adventures blog. So, here are my thoughts on cover letters.

My first big take away from the career workshops, particularly those run by recruiters themselves, was that cover letters are not typically even read. They may be glanced at before going on to the resume. However, if the cover letter is formatted in what's known as a T format, then they will get more than a glance and may be skimmed by the recruiter.

The T format cover letter is formatted into two columns. The first column covers the stated requirements of the job. The second column covers how your experience addresses each of those requirements. Since learning this little bit of information, I've always provided a T format cover letter. I will also note that the work you spend on this type of cover letter is a great way to get started in customizing your resume for each job application.

On the next page is an example of a cover letter that I created to apply for a communications leadership position. You can see the two-column approach with the key aspects of the job down the left hand column and then my matching skills and experience in the right hand column. Ideally, you're writing somewhat more concise descriptions of how you match the job. I'm afraid that my example may have been a bit long winded and due to the extra type wouldn't readily attract the recruiter to actually read it.

Another way that I was coached on cover letters was to include them as the first page of your resume in the file you submitted online. I like this approach a great deal. After all, you've spent a great deal of time on both the cover letter and the resume. You want to make sure that the recruiter and the hiring manager see all the pertinent information. Give that option consideration the next time you forward your cover letter and resume.

Jim Wilson   Communicator | Organizer | Builder

                                                                2605 Valleywood Drive
                                                                Grapevine, Texas 76051
                                                                682-217-4030 mobile
                                                                jbwilson@me.com

Date: 22 November 2013

Subject: Communications and Media Manager Search

I'm delighted to learn of your Communications and Media Manager search and feel strongly that I can readily meet and exceed your requirements. Here's a brief summary followed by my resume.

Communications Planning: I've worked at all levels of an organization, from executive board to major donors to frontline staff and volunteers, crafting and executing communication programs as well as branding initiatives. I establish measures and monitor progress toward goals, making adjustments when warranted.

Public Relations: I've served as communications and public relations director for the Boy Scouts of America driving their media relations, event press coverage, executive visibility program (including speech writing), and conducting press interviews.

Websites & Social Media: In my professional and volunteer roles I've developed websites and social media channels and implemented extensive promotional campaigns. I've personally built four websites using WordPress, including my blog on career topics at www.PathForeWord.com

Writing & Speaking: I'm an accomplished writer including textbooks, presentations, briefing books, case studies, executive speeches, and blogs. As a speaker I've been a college instructor (marketing and decision making) and presented to professional meetings.

Education: I've earned an MBA with concentrations in Marketing and Finance as well as an MA in Management. My undergraduate degree is in electronics.

While my past experience has been leading teams and departments, my recent volunteer work across several Scouting initiatives has been as both leader and individual contributor. At this stage of my career I welcome the prospect of rolling up my sleeves and directly making things happen to support the mission of the Center for Vital Longevity and the University of Texas at Dallas.

Please review my full range of qualifications via my resume on the next few pages. Then, let's talk!

                                                                        Continued...

Interview Tips

This is a compilation of previous posts on the topic of interviewing. It starts out about preparing your success stories, goes into questions that you can expect during your interview, questions you should ask, and ends by discussing how the interview process never really stops. I hope this provides insight for your job search PathForeWord.

STAR Stories

Much has been made recently about "behavioral interviewing". This technique asks you to describe specific examples of how you addressed key issues or projects during your previous employment. The fundamental premise is that what you've done in the past is the best predictor of your future results. It's a very sound way of conducting an interview. But it is not new.

I have stashed away in my employment files a series of articles published in the National Business Employment Weekly in the late 1980s. This printed weekly was published by the Wall Street Journal and contained all their employment ads for the previous week. How things have changed...

What hasn't changed is how best to prepare for those interviews. One of the articles is titled "Scripted Answers to Interview Questions". Another is sub-titled "Interviewers need to see future potential, not former titles". This last article goes into the S-T-A-R approach. This is the principle of building stories around previous Situations. The Task that you took on. The specific Actions that you took. And ends with the Results that you were able to achieve, ideally with measurements. I have usually combined the Task and the Action into a single action step.

The point is to look at the key competencies, skills, and experiences you need to excel in open position. Then prepare STAR stories that demonstrate those things in action — proving not only that you can do the job but that you have already done elements of the job and done so successfully. Having a short scripted response for each one can also help you feel confident in your message and ensure that you address the critical items of each story.

I'll note that when my daughter Kyla was interviewing for her first job after college. I coached her to first build the STAR stories and then use them in the interview. I noted that some interviewers will ask for specific examples that tie into the current job opening. I further noted that others will only ask general questions. The key is to use your STAR stories no matter what. If you're confronted with a general question, address that question and then transition into the most suitable STAR story to demonstrate how you've handled those situations in the past and will in the future. After the interview she noted that as she moved from office to office interviewing with several people, she confronted both approaches and was ready with her STAR stories to get the important message across — I can do this job, here's why.

Questions to Expect

These questions were developed for my own interviewing process, generally for candidates that had been previously qualified through skill testing and rigorous interviews by the direct hiring manager. My role was to provide a second or third interview that allowed the direct hiring manager to sit to one side and just watch. Typically, there would be two finalists and this was a great way to get the direct hiring manager off the spot, allowing them to really see the candidates in direct comparison.

With that framework in mind, I developed these questions not to pose technical issues or skills, but instead to see how well each candidate could think and communicate. Here's the key questions that I used during those sessions.

1. Tell me about yourself. Why did you choose this type of work?

2. What attracts you to this position? How does this position relate to your past work/career experience?

3. What things in your job do you feel that you have done particularly well, or in which you have achieved the greatest success? For what things have your managers complimented you?

4. What is the area in which you would most like to improve? What aspects of your previous jobs gave you the most trouble?

5. What was your biggest failure in your last job?

6. Wherever you worked before, what made it a good day?

7. What are some of the things you would like to avoid in a job and why?

8. How do you define teamwork? Give an example of a project that you have worked on that shows experience in working in a team environment.

9. What kind of people do you find most difficult to work with? How have you been successful in those situations?

10. Describe how you determine your priorities on your current job. Give me a specific example of how you schedule your time on an unusually hectic day.

11. Give me an example of a time when you had to go above and beyond the call of duty in order to get a job done.

12. What kind of person is your supervisor? What are your supervisor's greatest strengths? In what areas could they have done a better job?

13. If I were your supervisor, what would be the most important thing for me to say or do to support you?

14. If you were hiring someone for this job, what qualities would you look for?

15. Let's assume for a minute that you have one concern about accepting this job. What is that one concern?

16. Why should we hire you?

Questions to Ask

This section goes into the often overlooked aspect of what question you should ask of the interviewer. This is your opportunity to first surface any issues that the interviewer may have that you need to get out in the open and address. Second, you can learn more about the position, the organization, and the interviewer. And, third, it is your opportunity to impress the interviewer with your thoughtful questions. After all, your interviewer has already heard their questions and most of the answers before. It's your questions that will bring something new to the conversation.

On the first point above, I always like to ask if the interviewer has any concerns at this stage of the process.

This quite often surfaces some hidden concerns that are quietly resting below the surface and getting ready to send your prospects to the bottom of the ocean. Getting them out in the open allows the interviewer to candidly express them and allows you to address them. Don't ever pass up the opportunity to ask this most critical of questions. Of course, if the concern is truly a deal breaker that you can't overcome, it does help you prepare for your next interview…

Your key focus should be on the organization's needs. Then you can focus on how you can use your expertise, experience, and enthusiasm to meet those needs. Here's the list of questions that I've prepared as I get ready for an interview:

1. How did the opening occur?

2. What were the previous person's best attributes in the position? Any improvements you'd like to see?

3. What are the key goals for this position, for the organization?

4. What do you want accomplished in the first 60, 90, and 120 days?

5. What are the biggest stumbling blocks to expect?

6. Are there any gaps between what we've discussed and what you're seeking? Any concerns at this point?

7. What are the next steps in the search process?

That next to last question zeros in on one way of articulating the question — are there any concerns with me that I can address?

Interviewing Never Stops

Even after you've landed the job. Even after you've proven your value to your new organization. You're interviewing for your next position. That next position might be a step up. Or, it could be a step out of the organization.

I've always been amazed by the guys that would show up for a promotion interview with a new suit on. Of course, this showed that they were taking the interview seriously. But when they wore wrinkled khakis and polo shirts every day for the last several years, was the suit now really going to make a difference? Like it or not, they had already made an indelible impression on the hiring manager.

I'm also reminded of hearing a recent story about Southwest Airlines. The story goes that when they fly someone in for an interview, they ask their gate agents and stewards if this is someone who should be joining the Southwest team. In this case, the interview started before the candidate expected it to start.

Given all this, how about your references — will they be your champions when discussing your past job performance or your character? Haven't you been, in essence, interviewing with them for the past several years? Will they be able to honestly say that you're a great fit for the job? The same applies to past and current supervisors.

A friend of mine once told me about his organization where he would receive direct feedback from his supervisor based on his attendance at sales conferences. This wasn't about after meeting parties. Instead, it was detailed feedback about his work in meetings and how he could better participate, engage, and contribute. It was feedback compiled from many different observers from all levels of the organization and assembled for the express purpose of improving his current performance and preparing him for his next position. Depending on your viewpoint, it could be a superb performance evaluation system or an interviewing system with feedback. The point is, you're always under observation.

So, while you've been prepping for the interview, keep in mind that the effective presentation of you, your skills, and your operating style never, never ends. You're always on stage and constantly being evaluated by those around you — whether that is a formal evaluation or the informal categorization of who you are and where you might fit in the future of your organization.

In your PathForeWord, don't stop interviewing for that next job and to be the one selected to continue with your current job.

###

About Jim Wilson

I'm an advocate of lifelong learning. I often describe it as "just in time training". Throughout my life I've engaged in continuous improvement and learning. In my early career, I used home study courses (all paper and postage stamps in those days). Now I engage in online courses or looking up what I need at the time I need it. The Internet is just superb at facilitating this type of learning.

My formal education is a bachelor's degree in Electronics Engineering Technology, earned at age 35 primarily because I'd decided I needed graduate level education in my work as a manager and leader in the technical training and publishing industry. I earned a master of arts in management at age 37 followed by an MBA in finance at 42 and added the marketing concentration at 47. Of course, learning never stops but is achieved through hands-on experience, trial and error, and in my case with an emphasis on the latter...

I've been particularly blessed to work in industries and on tasks that I love. My early career was spent as a broadcast engineer, electronics instructor, home study course and textbook writer, editor and manager. My executive career began as a product line manager for a line of electronics training materials and went on to the role of corporate director of education for a chain of technical schools. Then I led a division focused on developing aviation training. I went on to lead publishing and communication for the Boy Scouts of America for twenty-one years, retiring in 2013.

At this point I'm "rewiring" rather than "retiring" and building a writing, consulting, and publishing/communication project business called PathForeWord. As part of that activity I write a career

focused blog at http://www.PathForeWord.com and I write
a blog on my amateur radio hobby at http://www.K5ND.net

I hope you find this book valuable and I invite you to check
in with my blogs or to contact me with questions or better
yet, answers!